S0-DGM-723

World Leaders

GEORGE BUSH

rourke biographies

World Leaders

GEORGE BUSH

by
WILLIAM E. PEMBERTON

Rourke Publications, Inc.
Vero Beach, Florida 32964

Copyright © 1993, by Rourke Publications, Inc.
All rights in this book are reserved. No part of this work
may be used or reproduced in any manner whatsoever or
transmitted in any form or by any means, electronic or
mechanical, including any information storage and retrieval
system, without written permission from the copyright
owner except in the case of brief quotations embodied in
critical articles and reviews. For information address the
publisher, Rourke Publications, Inc., P.O. Box 3328, Vero
Beach, Florida 32964.

∞ The paper used in this book conforms to the American
National Standard for Permanence of Paper for Printed
Library Materials, Z39.48-1984.

Library of Congress Cataloging-in-Publication Data
Pemberton, William E., 1940-
    George Bush / written by William E. Pemberton.
        p.   cm. — (Rourke biographies. World leaders)
    Includes bibliographical references and index.
    Summary: A biography of the forty-first president of the
United States, with emphasis on his background and life in
politics.
    ISBN 0-86625-478-1 (alk. paper)
    1. Bush, George, 1924-   —Juvenile literature. 2. Presi-
dents—United States—Biography—Juvenile literature.
[1. Bush, George, 1924-   . 2. Presidents.]   I. Title. II.
Series.
E882.P46   1993
973.928'092—dc20
[B]   92-46768
                                                    CIP
                                                    AC

PRINTED IN THE UNITED STATES OF AMERICA

Contents

Color Illustrations

World Leaders

GEORGE BUSH

Chapter 1

The Crisis of the 1990's

In January, 1989, George Bush was inaugurated as the forty-first president of the United States. Few previous presidents had seemed to be so well-prepared for that office. As a young man, Bush received a superb education, became a war hero, and earned a fortune in the Texas oil industry. Entering political life, he received practical training in the rough-and-tumble of Texas politics. He then served in national politics in a variety of ways: He was the U.S. ambassador to the United Nations, chair of the Republican National Committee, envoy to China, director of the Central Intelligence Agency (CIA), and vice president of the United States.

Being elected president seemed to be a fitting climax to Bush's many years of service to his country. The new president, however, quickly found that all of his experience would be needed to deal with the problems of the times—problems so serious that they have been called the "crisis of the 1990's."

Crises Before the 1990's

George Bush was certainly not the first president to face a difficult situation upon his election. A series of crises have shaped recent United States history, always testing the presidents who had to face them. For example, the "crisis of the 1890's" occurred when Americans first felt the full impact of industrialization. There was widespread unemployment, and violent protests and labor strikes resulted. These events gave birth to the progressive movement, which sought government action to improve the economic situation. Progressive reforms

A formal portrait of George Bush, the forty-first president of the United States. (White House Historical Association)

achieved by presidents Theodore Roosevelt and Woodrow Wilson helped solve the economic problems.

During the Great Depression of the 1930's, millions of Americans were without jobs or the hope of finding work. Led by President Franklin D. Roosevelt, the government began many new programs, such as the Works Progress Administration, Social Security, and unemployment insurance. These were designed to create jobs and to help those who were out of work.

In the late 1940's and early 1950's, the Cold War crisis began. At that time, just after World War II ended, the United States and the Soviet Union became the world's "superpowers." Both countries were armed with nuclear weapons, and each viewed the other as a frightening, dangerous enemy. The Cold War, as this standoff was called, caused President Harry S. Truman and the U.S. Congress to put the government and economy on a war footing that lasted for fifty years.

Crises such as these established some presidents, such as Theodore Roosevelt, Woodrow Wilson, Franklin D. Roosevelt, and Harry Truman, as major figures. However, they destroyed the presidencies of those such as William Howard Taft and Herbert Hoover who could not meet the challenge. Like these earlier presidents, President George Bush faced a crisis—a particularly trying one that would challenge his leadership in both foreign and domestic affairs.

The End of the Cold War

Crises in foreign affairs did not intimidate President Bush, who regarded Cold War diplomacy as his specialty. Since his early years in politics, the two superpowers had been prepared at a moment's notice to launch nuclear missile attacks upon each other. They also backed opposing sides in wars in such places as Korea, Vietnam, and Afghanistan.

13

The threat of World War III beginning between the superpowers ended during President Bush's administration. The Cold War had cost both the Soviet Union and the United States huge amounts of money, and the Soviet system finally buckled under the strain. Eastern Europe threw off Soviet control and held free elections. Soviet leader Mikhail Gorbachev stunned the world by ending Communist Party domination in the Soviet Union. Gorbachev pushed for dramatic reforms, attempting to rebuild the failing Soviet economy. Once set in motion, however, changes moved too quickly for him to control.

The republics that made up the Soviet Union were demanding independence, and central power weakened. Boris Yeltsin replaced Gorbachev as the most powerful figure in the country. Then, in late 1991, the Soviet Union itself was dissolved. Its republics became independent countries. President Bush declared that the Cold War was over and the United States had won.

Bush proclaimed that a new, peaceful, democratic world order was emerging. Yet even welcome change can be disturbing, and many worrisome questions remained. For example, what would happen to Soviet nuclear missiles as that nation disintegrated? Strong American and Soviet control over their allies was now ending. Would the world therefore witness an outbreak of civil wars and small wars between independent nations? In the poor countries of the world, hundreds of millions of people faced unimaginable poverty. Millions of people starved to death each year. What did the increasing gap in wealth between rich and poor nations mean for global stability and peace? President Bush used military force against Panamanian dictator Manuel Noriega in 1989 and Iraqi dictator Saddam Hussein in 1991. What did this say about the nature of peace and the role of the United States in the "new world order"?

Troubles Within the United States

At home, President Bush faced politically explosive challenges. Most domestic problems stemmed from changes in the economy. Beginning in the 1960's, the United States' domination of the world economy began to erode as countries that had been devastated by World War II in the 1940's recovered. Japan, Germany, and other nations began to claim an increasing share of the world market. Many experts suspected that the American economic decline stemmed from deeper problems. Some thought that by the 1990's, the United States had invested so much money in its military structure that the economic and social foundations of society were crumbling.

U.S. Presidents, 1897-1993

President	Years in Office	Political Party
William McKinley	1897-1901	Republican
Theodore Roosevelt	1901-1909	Republican
William Howard Taft	1909-1913	Republican
Woodrow Wilson	1913-1921	Democrat
Warren G. Harding	1921-1923	Republican
Calvin Coolidge	1923-1929	Republican
Herbert Hoover	1929-1933	Republican
Franklin D. Roosevelt	1933-1945	Democrat
Harry S. Truman	1945-1953	Democrat
Dwight D. Eisenhower	1953-1961	Republican
John F. Kennedy	1961-1963	Democrat
Lyndon B. Johnson	1963-1969	Democrat
Richard M. Nixon	1969-1974	Republican
Gerald R. Ford	1974-1977	Republican
Jimmy Carter	1977-1981	Democrat
Ronald Reagan	1981-1989	Republican
George Bush	1989-1993	Republican
Bill Clinton	1993-	Democrat

For years most people ignored such warnings. By the time President Bush won the election in 1988, however, millions of Americans were noticing changes in their lives. Statistics told the story. Beginning in 1947, Americans had lived through a long period of prosperity. This golden age ended in 1973. From 1973 to 1990, people's earnings (when adjusted to account for inflation) fell by 19.1 percent.

The American middle class found its prosperity eroding. People below the middle class were trapped there, with no ladder out. President Ronald Reagan took credit for the millions of new jobs created during his administration (1981-1989), but he ignored the fact that half of them paid below poverty-level wages. The number of high-paid manufacturing jobs steadily declined, replaced by low-paid service positions. In other words, employment at businesses such as McDonald's and Wendy's fast-food restaurants replaced jobs at Ford and General Motors. Social conditions quietly deteriorated. In 1990, the census bureau found that 33.6 million Americans (of a total population of 248.7 million) lived below the poverty line. The United States had the highest murder rate in the world and had one of the highest drug-crime rates.

The American political system seemed paralyzed. American leaders appeared to be helpless or unwilling to tackle these problems. They could not decide how to raise the hundreds of billions of dollars needed to rebuild the United States' economic and social structure. The country's schools and health systems were in a desperate condition.

Each crisis in recent United States history tested presidents; some passed, some failed. Few chief executives ever seemed so superbly prepared as George Bush to face such challenges. Yet few presidents had inherited such a deep and confusing crisis as that of the 1990's.

Chapter 2

Child of Privilege

George Bush is a fortunate man. Like Presidents Theodore and Franklin Roosevelt, he was born into the "Establishment." The Establishment refers to the relatively small number of American families with inherited wealth and influence; they are the American version of an aristocracy. Bush's family was well-to-do and socially elite. He had the best education available to Americans, and he had the intelligence to make good use of it. Although George Bush was born to wealth and privilege, however, he also could take pride in his own achievements. He attained success on his own as a war hero, an oil millionaire, and an important Texas politician.

George Herbert Walker, George Bush's maternal grandfather, was a fourth-generation American. His ancestors had come from England in the seventeenth century. He established a successful investment firm in St. Louis, Missouri, and built a huge summer home on Walker's Point in Kennebunkport, Maine. This home was inherited by George and Barbara Bush. George Bush's father's side of the family was also successful in business. The family goes back several generations in America and is connected through history to British royalty. George Bush is the thirteenth cousin, twice removed, of Queen Elizabeth.

Prescott and Dorothy Bush

Prescott S. Bush, George's father, was the most influential person in his son's life. In fact, George would eventually have to break from this imposing figure to keep from being overpowered. Prescott was born in Columbus, Ohio, in 1896.

He formed his connections with the Eastern Establishment by attending St. George's preparatory school in Newport, Rhode Island. In 1913 he entered Yale University, open at that time only to the children of the "best families." At Yale, Prescott achieved academic success, became captain of the baseball team, and was inducted into the prestigious secret society Skull and Bones. After graduation, he entered the business world and eventually became a partner in one of the nation's great investment banking houses, Brown Brothers, Harriman. George Herbert Walker, Prescott's father-in-law, was president of the company.

Prescott's success on Wall Street allowed him and his wife, Dorothy, to protect their five children from the harsh reality of life in the Great Depression of the 1930's. The Bush family lived in Greenwich, Connecticut, one of the richest communities in America. Prescott and Dorothy had a beautiful home, a cook, two maids, and a chauffeur. Prescott became wealthy but did not particularly enjoy business. He was involved in civic activities and then in politics. In 1952, at age fifty-five, he won election to the United States Senate. Prescott was a moderate Republican in the mold of Dwight D. Eisenhower, who was elected president that same year. He supported most of Franklin Roosevelt's social programs but wanted to limit their growth.

Dorothy Bush was also a major figure in shaping the personality and values of her son George. She infused him with competitive drive, self-discipline, and modesty. She showed him the importance of developing and maintaining relationships with other people, a valuable lesson for a future politician. She cultivated a gentle, empathic side to his nature. Once, during parents' day athletic events at his school, George saw a young overweight boy get trapped in a barrel on an obstacle course. He broke into tears at the sight of the boy's humiliation, helped him, and then finished the course with him.

18

Fifteen-year-old George Bush (left), a student at Phillips Academy, was a finalist in the Field Club's tournament. (AP/Wide World Photos)

Despite their wealth, Prescott and Dorothy taught George the old-fashioned Puritan values of self-discipline and hard work. His family imbued him with the Establishment sense of "noblesse oblige"—the belief that those who enjoy wealth and privilege have a duty and obligation to serve society. People who later wondered what Bush believed in had to look no further than this. It was no surprise to George when his father entered politics. "He'd made his mark in the business world," George Bush later said: "Now he felt he had a debt to pay."

Early Years

George Bush was born on June 12, 1924, while his parents were living temporarily in Milton, Massachusetts. Since his mother could not decide which of her father's names to give him, he became George Herbert Walker Bush. As a child he was given the nickname "Poppy," which fortunately he abandoned before he entered politics.

George lived in a neighborhood of wealthy and powerful families, attended private schools, and spent idyllic summers in Kennebunkport. Young George loved sports, and it was an interest that stayed with him throughout his life. He mastered tennis, golf, sailing, and fishing. Religion was another important part of his life. Prescott read Bible lessons to the family each morning, and the family attended church every Sunday.

George started school at the Greenwich Country Day School. Then, in 1936, when he was twelve, his parents sent him to a private boarding school, Phillips Academy (usually referred to as Andover) in Andover, Massachusetts. With nine hundred boys, Andover was one of the largest and best American preparatory schools for the children of the Establishment. It had a splendid art museum, a superb scientific laboratory, and a library superior to that of many colleges.

It had its shortcomings, however. It placed more emphasis on work and discipline than on creativity. Also, Andover boys were from similar backgrounds: wealthy, established, white families. There were few scholarship boys at Andover and fewer nonwhites. Within these limits, Andover boys were given a fine education, with emphasis on the tradition of noblesse oblige.

George Bush's teachers recalled that he was more industrious than brilliant, but through hard work he won honors in scholarship and sports. He was president of his senior class and captain of the baseball and soccer teams. Nor did he neglect his social life. During his senior year, George attended a Christmas dance at the Round Hill Country Club in Greenwich. He saw a lively and pretty brunette and arranged an introduction. This was Barbara Pierce, who would later become his wife.

Most of his classmates scattered into the Ivy League universities when they graduated from Andover in 1942. World War II was raging, however, and George decided to enter the Navy. He served until 1945; after his discharge, he entered Yale University.

Barbara Bush

On January 6, 1945, before he entered Yale, George married Barbara Pierce. After they met as teenagers, Barbara and George never developed a serious romantic interest in anyone else. Barbara said she married the first man she kissed. Barbara was born on June 8, 1925, and her background was similar to George's. Her father was an executive and later chairman of the board of McCall Corporation, a large magazine publisher. She developed close ties with her father, but her mother was a controlling person, obsessed with "proper" behavior. Their relationship was not close.

Barbara followed her mother's wishes—and escaped her

clutches—by attending a finishing school, Ashley Hall, in South Carolina. She then went to Smith College, an elite women's college in Massachusetts. Rejection of her mother's pretensions enabled Barbara to develop the down-to-earth personality that later would make her one of the most popular American women of her time.

Barbara Bush began married life at a time in American history when gender roles were slowly beginning to change. As increasing numbers of women entered the work force,

George and Barbara Bush in 1945, not long after they were married. They met when they were teenagers. (AP/Wide World Photos)

Barbara stayed at home in the traditional role of wife and mother. That role could sometimes be stifling. She later said of her early years with George, "In a marriage where one is so willing to take on responsibility and the other so willing to keep the bathrooms clean, that's the way you get treated." Finally, by the mid-1970's, she had gained the confidence she needed to establish an independent role for herself. Barbara

GEORGE BUSH

later won admiration because of her honest, direct approach to life. For example, many people liked her apparent lack of concern over her gray hair and wrinkles. She symbolized the traditional values of self-discipline, lack of pretention, and a stable family life.

Barbara and George Bush have much in common. They were both children of privilege, products of the American Establishment. They were not content, however, to rest on their family names and wealth. Their parents had taught them the work ethic: the value and dignity of hard work and self-discipline. They shared a sense of duty to serve society in return for their privileges. Finally, they both needed to escape powerful parents to achieve success on their own.

Chapter 3

The Self-Made Man

Young people born into families with wealth and high social status have many advantages. They sometimes suffer psychologically, however, because they lack the opportunity to gain pride and self-esteem through their own achievements. This was not the case with George Bush. He had the advantages, but, as a young adult, he also achieved personal success. He became a war hero in World War II. When he returned home, he was successful in business and politics in Texas, far from his New England family.

The War Hero

World War II started in Europe in 1939. While world attention focused on German dictator Adolf Hitler and the war in Europe, tension was increasing between the United States and Japan, as they struggled for domination of the Pacific. On December 7, 1941, Japan attacked American forces at Pearl Harbor in the Hawaiian Islands. The United States then declared war on both Germany and Japan.

Bush finished his senior year at Andover and, in 1942, joined the Navy Air Corps. In June, 1943, he received his wings and became a bomber pilot; he was only eighteen years old. Bush trained to fly the Avenger torpedo bomber. It was one of the largest aircraft carrier-based airplanes in the world, with a fifty-four-foot wing span. It was a slow, sturdy airplane that dropped its bombs from a steep downward glide pattern. Bush was assigned to the aircraft carrier USS *San Jacinto*, which joined the Pacific fleet in the early spring of 1944. On May 23, he had his first experience in combat when he flew attacks against Japanese installations on Wake Island.

One of his most frightening experiences came on June 19, when Japanese airplanes attacked the American fleet. With the *San Jacinto* under attack, its captain was too busy taking evasive movements to allow Bush to take off. Bush had to wait on deck for a tense thirty minutes in his fully exposed airplane, loaded with two thousand pounds of TNT. If his plane had been hit, he and many other Americans would have died in a gigantic explosion. When he got into the air, something went wrong—his airplane was either hit by gunfire or

Bush piloted a bomber in the Pacific in World War II. In July, 1944, he flew thriteen air strikes. (AP/Wide World Photos)

malfunctioned. Bush set the big bomber down in the water. He and his two crew members anxiously watched the rest of the battle from a life raft until they were rescued.

In July Bush flew thirteen air strikes. In August, his task force moved to the Bonin Islands. These heavily fortified islands, which included Iwo Jima and Chichi Jima, were strategically important to Japan's defense.

On September 2, 1944, Commander Don Melvin led Bush and the other members of his Avenger squadron in an attack on a radio tower on Chichi Jima. As they arrived over the small island in the early morning light, Bush pushed the nose of his bomber into a thirty-degree dive, following two other airplanes to the target. Suddenly, antiaircraft fire hit his bomber. The controls turned sluggish and the cockpit filled with smoke. Bush saw fire race out along the wings toward the gasoline tanks. He managed to keep the burning airplane steady. The pilots behind him later reported that all four of his five-hundred-pound bombs hit the tower.

Adrift in a Life Raft

Bush pulled out of the dive and flew over the water. He decided that the airplane was too badly damaged either to get back to the carrier or to land on the water. He radioed his two crewmen to bail out but received no reply. Later reports said that one of the men did jump, but both died. Bush bailed out, but his parachute snarled on the plane's tail assembly, and the rear wing hit his head.

His damaged parachute opened, and Bush hit the water, dazed but conscious. American pilots circled overhead, trying to help him. One pilot signaled him, indicating where his self-inflating raft was floating, and Bush swam to it. Another pilot dropped a medical kit for his head injury. He had been stung by jellyfish and was sick from swallowing sea water. Unfortunately, the other pilots had to return to the carrier and

A Month on the *Finback*

I still don't understand the 'logic' of war—why some survive and others are lost in their prime. But that month on the Finback gave me time to reflect, to go deep inside myself and search for answers. As you grow older and try to retrace the steps that made you the person you are, the signposts to look for are those special times of insight, even awakening. I remember my days and nights aboard the U.S.S. Finback as one of those times—maybe the most important of them all. (George Bush, *Looking Forward*)

leave him alone at sea. Bush was scared. He feared being washed back to the island, rumored to be a place of horrors for prisoners of war. Yet a terrible death surely awaited him if he were to be swept away from the island and lost at sea.

For nearly two hours, the injured, frightened young man struggled to maintain his position. Then he faced a new terror. A submarine periscope thrust from beneath the water. Was it Japanese or American? Bush cried with relief when the USS *Finback*, a 311-foot submarine, surfaced, and its crew members pulled him to safety. For a month, Bush lived on the cramped submarine. He often went on deck alone at night, when the vessel surfaced under the protection of darkness. He thought about his dead comrades. Bush, a deeply religious man, believed that he had lived because he had a mission on earth.

After a month, the *Finback* returned to port and Bush rejoined his carrier. He flew a few more missions, then in December, 1944, returned to the United States. He got to spend the holidays with his family and with Barbara, to whom he had been engaged before entering the Navy. George and Barbara were married two weeks later, in January, 1945. She then joined him until the Navy discharged him in September of that year. Bush had logged 1,228 hours of flying time, made

126 carrier landings, and flown fifty-eight missions. He had also won a Distinguished Flying Cross and three air medals.

Going to College

In September, 1945, when Bush was discharged, the war was over. Many young men were heading for college and trying to make up for lost time. In keeping with his upbringing in the eastern Establishment, Bush went to Yale University. A classmate, future Senator John H. Chafee, recalled George as a "golden boy." He was already a standout among these young men, many of whom would emerge as the nation's economic, professional, and political leaders. Bush majored in economics and won academic honors. He also was inducted into the

At Yale, Bush excelled in both academics and sports. He was captain of the baseball team. (AP/Wide World Photos)

> **Moving West**
>
> *I didn't want to do anything pat and predictable. I'd come of age in a time of war, seen different people and cultures, known danger, and suffered the loss of close friends. . . . The world I'd known before the war didn't interest me. I was looking for a different kind of life, something challenging, outside the established mold. I couldn't see myself being happy commuting into work, then back home, five days a week.* (George Bush, *Looking Forward*)

exclusive Skull and Bones club and won letters in baseball and soccer. Bush played first base and was captain of the baseball team.

The Bushes lived off-campus in crowded student housing, in an old house converted into apartments. In 1946, Barbara gave birth to their first child, George Walker Bush. George was now both a college student and a father. He worked hard and, as many eager former servicemen did, finished college in two and a half years.

The Texas Oilman

In 1948 George Bush was graduated from Yale. He and Barbara were not sure what they wanted to do, but George knew that he did not want to settle back into the comfortable routine of life that he had led before the war. Barbara later admitted that they also wanted to get away from their overpowering parents.

George had saved three thousand dollars, and in the summer of 1948 they left for the "oil patch" in West Texas. There they joined in the oil frenzy with other young people. "There wasn't anything subtle or complicated about it," George later wrote: "We all just wanted to make a lot of money quick." A family friend, Neil Mallon, the president of Dresser Industries, hired George to work in a Dresser oil subsidiary. Bush swept hot, dusty warehouses, painted oil pumps, and did anything else that needed doing.

Instead of moving up slowly in Dresser, George decided to take a different route. In 1951 he and a neighbor, John Overbey, formed their own independent oil company. Two years later, Bush and Overbey joined two brothers, Hugh and William Liedtke, to form Zapata Petroleum. Hugh Liedtke was president and ran the company, with George Bush as vice president.

Hugh Liedtke was already becoming a local legend. Under his leadership, Zapata drilled 127 oil wells without a dry hole. Throughout his life, Bush had a knack for allying himself with capable and ambitious people. Hugh and George formed a subsidiary, Zapata Off-Shore, to drill for oil in the Gulf of Mexico. In 1959 they decided to divide the company. George took over Zapata Off-Shore and moved to Houston.

While George was achieving business success, he and Barbara were also busy raising a big family: George Walker (born in 1946), Robin (1949), John Ellis (1953), Neil Mallon (1955), Marvin Pierce (1956), and Dorothy (1959). There also was tragedy in their lives, however. Robin died from leukemia when she was only four years old.

By the mid-1960's, Bush had become one of a legendary group of Texas oil millionaires. Money, however, had never been his life's goal. Wealth was a source of freedom that would allow him to pursue other ends. In 1966 George decided to sell Zapata Off-Shore and leave the business world. This closed an important phase of George Bush's life. He had accumulated a fortune that gave him the independence needed to devote his time and energy to public service. He had a big family that gave him continuing emotional support. His success had also reinforced some basic ingredients in the Bush personality: healthy self-esteem, optimism, and confidence.

Chapter 4

Success in Public Service

In 1962 Republican leaders asked George Bush to chair the party in Harris County, where Houston was located. He quickly agreed: "This was the challenge I'd been waiting for—an opening into politics at the ground level, where it all starts." He chose the path Prescott Bush had followed years before, leaving the business world for public service.

Entry into Politics

From the beginning of his political career, Bush showed that he was not an ideological politician. In other words, he was never guided by a deeply held, rigid system of social and economic ideas. Bush called himself a conservative, but since he was not guided by a strong set of political principles, he changed his positions as times changed. Political terms such as conservative (or "right") and liberal (or "left") are difficult to define. Conservative politicians tend to oppose powerful, expensive government. Liberals tend to support the use of government programs to deal with such social and economic problems as poverty and racial discrimination. "Moderate" politicians are neither far right nor far left; they often combine elements of conservatism and liberalism.

Bush worked hard to build the Republican Party in Texas. He was one of many young men and women who were bringing new life to the party in the South and Southwest, breaking the century-long Democratic Party monopoly on the region. After watching Bush work successfully for two years as county chair, party leaders recruited him to run for the U.S. Senate against Democrat Ralph Yarborough in 1964.

Bush and his family in Texas in 1964, the year he first ran for the U.S. Senate. (AP/Wide World Photos)

In 1964 public attention was focused on the presidential
race between liberal Texas Democrat Lyndon Johnson and
conservative Republican Barry Goldwater of Arizona.
Goldwater's views were considered "far right." Bush ran for
the Senate as a Goldwaterite. He opposed the newly enacted
Civil Rights Act, attacked the United Nations, and supported
the Vietnam War. Bush ran a strong campaign but lost.

Bush later said that he learned two things from his early
political career. First, he found that "jugular" politics—the
vicious grab for an opponent's throat—made him uneasy.
Second, he realized that his hunger for victory had caused him
to distort his beliefs. He told his Episcopal minister in
Houston: "You know, John, I took some of the far right
positions to get elected. I hope I never do it again. I regret it."
Bush would shift his political positions in the future, however.
After 1964 he moved from the conservative camp into the
moderate wing of the Republican Party. He then shifted back
to the right in the years of Ronald Reagan's conservative
presidency, from 1981 to 1989.

The House of Representatives

In 1966 Bush ran for the House of Representatives in a
district located in a white, affluent section of Houston. He won
easily. Members of the House of Representatives are elected
every two years, and Bush won again in 1968. In the House,
Republican leaders gave Bush important assignments and
prepared him for leadership. He enjoyed the activity, the
ability to help people in his district, and the invitations to
campaign for friends in other parts of the country.

In 1970 Bush decided to give up his safe House seat and
run again for the Senate, this time against Lloyd Bentsen.
President Richard Nixon, who had been elected in 1968, came
to Texas and campaigned for Bush. Years later, Nixon aide
Charles Colson said that Nixon's people had found derogatory

information about Bentsen. Bush, however, thought he was winning and refused to "go negative" by using the information. Bentsen won narrowly. Bush's second defeat for the Senate threatened his political future. Fortunately, he had the support of President Nixon. Nixon helped him rebuild his career, which then blossomed under Presidents Gerald Ford and Ronald Reagan.

The United Nations

After the 1970 defeat, Nixon named Bush United States ambassador to the United Nations. Bush spent 1971 and 1972 at United Nations headquarters in New York. He gained new knowledge of foreign affairs, which became his special interest in politics. George and Barbara enjoyed the social whirl of diplomatic life. They used the endless round of dinners, parties, and receptions for foreign dignitaries to establish friendships with important figures from all over the world. During times of crisis when he became president, Bush personally would telephone world leaders asking for support for his policies. His friendships with many of these leaders began at the United Nations.

The Republican National Committee

Nixon won reelection easily in 1972. Nixon was always suspicious of possible enemies, and he brought people loyal to him into top positions. Nixon asked Bush to become chair of the Republican National Committee (RNC), the central body that directed the party. Bush accepted, although Barbara perceptively warned that it was an unrewarding job that would involve opening a "can of worms."

The can of worms turned out to be the Watergate scandal. It began during President Nixon's 1972 election campaign against his Democratic opponent, George McGovern. On June 17, 1972, five agents of the Nixon Committee to Reelect the President were arrested while breaking into the Democratic National Headquarters in the Watergate apartment complex in Washington, D.C. Investigations of Watergate uncovered many other White House crimes and "dirty tricks" against Nixon opponents. Nixon firmly denied any knowledge of these activities. Eventually, about twenty Nixon associates went to prison.

As the crimes were uncovered, Nixon steadily lost support as more people began to believe he was lying. Increasingly, members of Congress began to call for his impeachment and removal from office. As the noose tightened around Nixon's neck, he still insisted that he had no knowledge of the crimes. He said to Bush, "George, I'm telling the truth." Bush believed him.

Bush was in a difficult position. He was loyal to Nixon, yet as RNC chair he was caretaker of the entire Republican Party. The party seemed to be endangered by the seemingly endless investigations. He wrote to a friend: "Watergate was the product of the actions of a few misguided, very irresponsible individuals who violated a high trust and who served neither the President nor their country well." Finally, Nixon's own secret tape recordings of conversations in his White House office revealed that he had engaged in a cover-up of a crime. The cover-up was itself a criminal action. Impeachment proceedings were already underway; Nixon's support, even among Republicans, melted away.

Bush's loyalty to Nixon almost cost him his career. Not until August 7, 1974, did Bush write to Nixon that it was time to resign. On August 9 Nixon finally did so. Feeling betrayed by Nixon's lies, Bush later told a friend: "I wouldn't care if I never see Richard Nixon again."

Envoy to China
Gerald Ford had been Richard Nixon's vice president; when

Nixon resigned, he became the new president. He offered Bush his choice of two prized assignments: the ambassadorship to England or to France. Bush surprised everyone by choosing instead to become the chief of the U.S. Liaison Office in China. He held this position throughout 1975.

He chose the post partly because he wanted to learn firsthand about a country that he thought was emerging as one of the world's major powers. Also, Beijing was thousands of miles away from Washington. It seemed a good place to be while problems associated with Watergate still rocked the capital. Yet in China, Bush felt as if he were in political exile. He wrote to a friend: "I'm sitting out here trying to figure out what to do with my life."

The Central Intelligence Agency

In late 1975, President Ford asked Bush to become director of the Central Intelligence Agency (CIA). The CIA is a powerful agency that gathers secret information about governments and military activities all over the world. Bush later described being CIA director as the best job in Washington, but when Ford offered him the job he was not sure he wanted it. He wanted a political career, and the CIA was supposed to be free of politics. The agency was also in trouble—a sinking ship, some people said.

Ford needed a loyal, competent CIA director who could heal the damaged agency. The CIA was in deep trouble. The nation had undergone years of bitter division caused by widespread opposition to the war in Vietnam, followed by the Watergate scandals. Many Americans had come to distrust all government institutions, especially those that operated in secret. Both the House and Senate had investigated CIA operations before Bush took charge. Congress found a pattern of illegal activity, including secret operations to damage the antiwar movement, surveillance of American journalists, and assassination attempts against foreign leaders.

On January 27, 1976, the Senate confirmed Bush to head the CIA. Bush was the right man to take control of the damaged agency. He was a loyal team player. He appeared to be open to the people and willing to cooperate with Congress. He testified fifty-one times before congressional committees during his year as director. By helping put the CIA back on its feet, he showed a key characteristic of his public career: He was a good caretaker of government institutions.

In November, 1976, Democrat Jimmy Carter defeated Gerald Ford for the presidency. Bush tried to get Carter to keep him on at the CIA, but Carter refused and replaced him in January, 1977. George and Barbara returned to Houston. They left thousands of friends and admirers waiting for them to reenter public life.

Bush being sworn in as director of the CIA in 1976; President Gerald Ford is at the right. (AP/Wide World Photos)

Chapter 5

The Vice Presidency

Back in Houston, Bush joined the boards of directors of several large firms. Business life, however, did not satisfy his need for public service. He looked for an opportunity to reenter politics. He decided to run for the most important office in the country: the presidency.

The Problem of Vision

If he hoped to become president, Bush had to put forward a vision of the nation's future that people could understand and support. He found that task difficult to accomplish. Bush himself once revealed his weakness in this area when he offhandedly dismissed the whole concept of "the vision thing."

Why did Bush find it difficult to develop a vision to place before the American people? For one thing, he was not a "man of the people." George Bush had never faced the problems that many average Americans confront every day: the stress of not having enough money to pay all the bills, the dreary monotony of dead-end jobs, the worry of paying for their children's education and medical care, the fear of not having enough savings to provide for a decent retirement. Most modern presidents had faced some of these problems, at least early in their careers; Bush had not.

Another problem Bush faced in expressing a vision was a division within the Republican Party itself. There were bitter arguments between two types of conservatives—the Eastern Establishment conservatives and the Western conservatives. The Eastern conservatives, for example, somewhat reluctantly accepted social programs and civil rights laws. Western conservatives, however, wanted to cut spending on social programs (especially those for the poor) and tended to oppose the push for civil rights. Western conservatives were also more aggressive in their desire to free business from government regulations.

George Bush, born in the East but living in Texas, was torn between these two forces within his party. He avoided choosing between them, so he could not formulate a system of ideas and programs—a "vision." Instead, Bush based his leadership on his competence as a manager. He was admired for his ability to manage governmental bodies well, to heal damaged organizations, and to deal effectively with crises.

The 1980 Campaign

On May 1, 1979, Bush announced his candidacy for the presidency. As the 1980 campaign opened, most experts believed that former California governor Ronald Reagan had the Republican nomination locked up. However, in Iowa's early 1980 contest (called the Iowa caucus) to choose the state's Republican nominee, Bush shocked the experts by defeating Reagan.

This startling victory spurred Reagan to action. Ronald Reagan was a strongly conservative politician and former actor from the West who had become a political force by articulating a powerful vision of America's future; Bush could not do that. Reagan hit the next primary at full speed and never slowed. His vision and his commanding presence, honed by his years of acting in motion pictures, paid off. He defeated Bush easily. As they moved on to other primaries, Bush fought Reagan hard and landed telling blows. He labeled Reagan's economic program, which combined tax reductions and high military spending, "voodoo economics," a tag that stuck. Yet Bush could not break the magnetic Reagan's hold on voters. Bush finally withdrew from the race.

One evening, as George and Barbara Bush sat discussing what they were going to do with the rest of their lives, the telephone rang. It was Ronald Reagan, who asked Bush if he would run as his vice president. Bush barely hesitated before making his decision: Yes. Bush surprised many people by quickly changing his stand on issues to match those of Reagan. He dropped his support for women's choice on abortion decisions and for a constitutional amendment guaranteeing equal rights for women. He now supported Reagan's economic policy. These changes did not seem particularly important to Bush, since he had never been an issue-oriented politician.

In November, 1980, Reagan and Bush easily defeated President Jimmy Carter and Vice President Walter Mondale. Four years later, in 1984, they won reelection for a second term against Walter Mondale and vice presidential candidate Geraldine Ferraro.

The Vice Presidency

The Reagan White House was divided between traditional Eastern conservatives and the new, Reaganite conservatives. The suspicious Reaganites regarded Bush as a moderate—or worse yet, perhaps even a liberal. They thought of him as an enemy in the Reagan camp. Bush realized that to succeed he would have to win Reagan's trust. He worked hard to establish a friendship with the president and never publicly disagreed with him, even in small meetings. Bush slowly gained Reagan's trust.

In March, 1981, a mentally disturbed young man named John Hinckley fired six shots into the presidential party as it was leaving a Washington hotel. One bullet struck Reagan and lodged an inch from his heart. The wound was serious, and it took weeks for the president to recover fully. In the meantime, Bush kept the government running smoothly and calmed national and international fears. He won Reagan's gratitude

From left to right, George and Barbara Bush and Nancy and Ronald Reagan. (AP/Wide World Photos)

and admiration by his quiet competence.

The United States Constitution assigns the vice president few important duties. The vice president's role depends on the president's wishes. President Reagan made George Bush an active partner in the administration. He gave Bush important assignments, including heading the White House crisis management team, overseeing aspects of international antidrug enforcement activities, and reforming government rules that regulate business, labor, and the environment. Bush often acted as a stand-in for the president at important functions. He spent over half of his time as vice president outside Washington, D.C., visiting all fifty states and nearly seventy foreign countries.

The Reagan Legacy

Ronald Reagan, president for two full terms, was one of the most popular presidents in the twentieth century. Under his leadership, the federal government cut taxes, reduced restrictions on business activity, and increased defense spending. These programs fueled economic expansion that benefited many people. As the Cold War with the Soviet Union began to wind down toward the end of Reagan's administration, the American people looked forward to peace as well as prosperity.

George Bush benefited from his association with the "Reagan Revolution." There were drawbacks, however. Two scandals that occurred during the Reagan years later threatened to hurt Bush's career. These were the near-collapse of the savings and loan (S&L) industry and the Iran-Contra scandal.

The Savings and Loan Disaster

Savings and loan associations had traditionally specialized in financing home mortgages. In the 1970's and 1980's, the government loosened regulation of the S&L's to make them more competitive with banks. Then, in 1982, the Reagan administration deregulated them almost entirely. Greedy people running many S&L's took advantage of the new freedom to make billions of dollars' worth of risky, foolish investments and loans in an attempt to turn a quick profit.

As president, Bush signs the bill to "bail out" the savings and loan industry from the crisis which began under President Reagan. (AP/WideWorld Photos)

They knew that, even if the investments went bad, the government would help them out. By 1988, greed had drained hundreds of S&L's, which were on the verge of failure. Although most of the damage occurred during the Reagan administration, the government did not act on the problem. The crisis therefore threatened Bush, who, as president, had to devise the expensive plan to save the system and safeguard investors' money.

The near collapse of the S&L system was a huge financial disaster for the United States government. The Bush administration "bailout" plan, by which the federal government assumed the losses suffered by failed S&L's, will amount to at least $500 billion over a thirty-year period; it may even be double that amount.

43

Iran-Contra

Another scandal that later returned to haunt Bush involved secret, illegal dealings by the Reagan administration that became known as the "Iran-Contra" scandal. Iran-Contra developed from several events that were occurring simultaneously.

Iran, controlled by anti-American followers of the Ayatollah Khomeini, was in a long and deadly war with Iraq. Halfway around the world, in central America, the Nicaraguan government was in the hands of the Sandinista political party. The Reagan administration thought of the Sandinista government as a Communist government, and therefore as the United States' enemy. President Reagan backed a group of Nicaraguan rebels called the Contras, who were trying to overthrow the Sandinistas.

The United States was giving money to support the Contras. Then Congress, trying to prevent further interference in the affairs of an independent nation, outlawed any further funding. Knowing that Reagan wanted the Contras to continue fighting, CIA Director William Casey, National Security Council (NSC) head John Poindexter, and NSC staff member Oliver North conspired to get around the ban.

The Reagan administration secretly sold arms to Iran in return for the release of American hostages held by anti-American groups in the Middle East. The Reagan people then gave the profits from the arms deal to the Contras. These secret dealings, and the cover-up that followed, broke American laws. As investigations began to reveal these activities, many Americans were outraged.

The problem for George Bush was that, as vice president, he was involved in the highest levels of government, and many people later wondered how much he had known about Iran-Contra. He insisted that he was "out of the loop" and did not know about the illegal dealings. Nevertheless, some people have alleged that he was aware of the Iran-Contra activities. Years later, in the last days of Bush's 1992 run for reelection, notes that had been taken at meetings by Reagan's secretary of defense, Caspar Weinberger, were made public. According to one note, Bush was present during at least one meeting at which the deal was being discussed.

Despite potential future problems from these events, the vice presidential years were good ones for Bush. He was in the inner circle of a popular administration and gained new experience at the top of government. He expanded his network of friends, who were ready to help him as he took his next big step to the top.

Chapter 6

Bush Wins the Presidency

As Ronald Reagan's second term ended, George Bush was sixty-four years old and was a nationally known figure. The 1988 election would be his best chance at the presidency, and he seized his opportunity.

Bush Seeks the Nomination

When Bush began the grueling round of state primaries in early 1988, political experts named him the front-runner for the Republican nomination. This helped him dominate press coverage and raise campaign funds, but it also meant that his opponents could focus their attacks on him. His major opponent for the nomination was Senator Robert Dole of Kansas.

Bush took the early contest in Iowa for granted, but Dole dealt him a humiliating defeat. This loss shocked Bush into action. He began to campaign hard, waging a negative campaign against Dole: Instead of explaining his own positions on issues, Bush attacked his opponent's weaknesses in well-crafted television advertisements. Momentum shifted back to Bush, and his well-financed campaign began to pay off. Bush won the important New Hampshire primary election in February, then more primaries. One opponent after another, including Dole, withdrew as they ran out of money and support. Weeks before the primary season ended, Bush secured the Republican nomination.

The Democrats held their convention in July; they chose Massachusetts governor Michael Dukakis as their nominee. After the convention, which gave Dukakis national exposure, opinion polls placed him far ahead of Bush. Bush, although vice president in a popular administration, simply did not have the appeal of President Reagan. His future depended on how he would present himself at the Republican Convention in New Orleans in August.

As the Republican Convention opened, he chose Indiana Senator Dan Quayle as his running mate. Unfortunately, the ill-prepared Quayle quickly proved to be an embarrassment. When he came under intense national scrutiny, Quayle became stiff and awkward, making verbal mistakes that created even closer scrutiny and then more mistakes.

Bush, however, did well at the convention, giving the best speech of his life. He stressed the Reagan legacy of peace and prosperity and said his goal was to complete the mission that Reagan began in 1980. He promised a new emphasis on environmental and educational reform. He also promised that there would be no new taxes:

> My opponent won't rule out raising taxes. But I will, and the Congress will push me to raise taxes, and I'll say no, and they'll push, and I'll say no, and they'll push again. And I'll say to them, "Read my lips, no new taxes."

Bush promised a better America: "I hope to stand for a new harmony, a greater tolerance. We've come far, but I think we need a new harmony among the races in our country." He said that America is "a brilliant diversity spread like stars, like a thousand points of light in a broad and peaceful sky." In a famous phrase, he said that he cared about those Americans who were struggling: "I want a kinder and gentler nation."

Running Against Dukakis

Bush came out of the convention with renewed energy and momentum. In some ways, however, he had trapped himself and limited his choices in the months and years ahead. First, he tied himself to Reagan's ideas and policies. This limited his ability to strike out in new directions. Then he made the popular promise that he would never raise taxes. This would further limit new programs, since there would be no additional money to pay for them.

Therefore, instead of using the fall campaign to explain how he would create a "kinder and gentler" America, Bush emphasized personality. Again using negative ads, he attacked Dukakis. Dukakis, on the advice of legal experts, had vetoed a Massachusetts bill to require teachers to lead students each day in the pledge of allegiance. Bush ads portrayed Dukakis as unpatriotic. In addition, the Massachusetts prison system had

In the 1988 election campaign, Bush shakes hands with Democratic nominee Michael Dukakis at the second debate. (AP/WideWorld Photos)

1. George and Barbara Bush enjoy the celebration after his acceptance speech at the 1988 Republican convention. At left are Marilyn and Dan Quayle. (AP/Wide World Photos)

2. George Bush (left) at the television debates with Democratic candidate Michael Dukakis in 1988. (AP/Wide World Photos)

3. George and Barbara Bush and Marilyn and Dan Quayle at the inauguration day
   ceremonies, January 20, 1989. (AP/Wide World Photos)

4. Three weeks after winning the 1988 election, Bush announces three members of
   his cabinet at a press conference. (AP/Wide World Photos)

5. President Bush meeting Soviet President Gorbachev. (AP/Wide World Photos)

6. President Bush delivers his State of the Union address, January 31, 1990. The positive
   events of 1989, he said, marked the "beginning of a new era in the world's affairs."
   (AP/Wide World Photos)

7. President Bush in the White House's famous Oval Office. (AP/Wide World Photos)

8. President Bush (clapping) welcomes world leaders to an economic summit in Houston, Texas, in July, 1990. From left: European Community President Delors, Italian Prime Minister Andreotti, West German Chancellor Kohl, French President Mitterrand, U.S. President Bush, British Prime Minister Thatcher, Canadian Prime Minister Mulroney, and Japanese Prime Minister Kaifu. (AP/Wide World Photos)

9. In Madrid, Spain, President Bush and Soviet President Gorbachev meet before convening Middle East peace talks in 1991. (AP/Wide World Photos)

10. President Bush visiting U.S. troops in Dhahran, Saudi Arabia, during the military buildup of Operation Desert Shield. (AP/Wide World Photos)

11. Campaigning in 1992, President Bush poses with children wearing traditional Polish costumes. (AP/Wide World Photos)

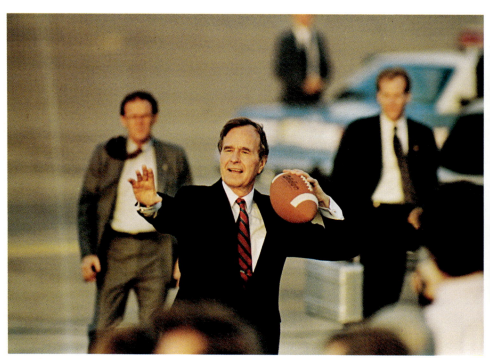

12. The former college athlete takes time out to toss a football. (AP/Wide World Photos)

13. President Bush greets the crowd outside his family's home in Kennebunkport, Maine. (AP/Wide World Photos)

14. George and Barbara Bush surrounded by their children, children's spouses, and
grandchildren. (AP/Wide World Photos)

released a convicted murderer named Willie Horton for a weekend. Horton fled and later raped a woman. Bush television spots used this to portray Dukakis as "soft" on crime.

Bush narrowed Dukakis' lead, then overtook him. The governor always seemed on the defensive, answering Bush's attacks instead of spelling out his stand on the issues. On November 8, 1988, Bush won the election, with 48,900,000 votes to 41,800,000 for Dukakis—53 percent to 46 percent of the popular vote.

Preparing for the Presidency

During the three months before his inauguration on January 20, 1989, George Bush began to plan for his presidency. He quickly worked to heal the wounds caused by the hard-fought, divisive election campaign. The American people now had a chance to see the George Bush that his friends knew: the happy, well-mannered, secure family man. Americans learned why even his opponents usually regarded Bush as a thoroughly nice and decent man.

Bush also used the three months of calm before his inauguration to select people for high government positions. This was a satisfying time for him. Years of hard work and service to the nation had paid off. Yet even an optimist such as George Bush must have wondered at times exactly what he had won. Even before he took office, Bush began to confront the crisis of the 1990's, which would shape Bush's next four years.

The Difficult Times Ahead

The world was changing rapidly, and the changes held both promise and great uncertainty. The Cold War was ending; fears of nuclear war, which had haunted the world since the late 1940's, were decreasing. Yet because the United States' and Soviet Union's control of the globe was slipping, there were more small conflicts and civil wars around the world. The world that Bush would face as president was suddenly quite different from the one he had spent so many years studying.

Within the United States, there was uncertainty over what to do about problems that had been quietly building for many years. Critics of American schools said that the country's educational system was one of the worst among all industrialized nations. Just as bad, American schoolchildren faced high levels of poverty and crime. Many things that had been built in the past, such as bridges, roads, buildings, and sewage systems, were crumbling and needed expensive repairs—physical structures such as these are sometimes called the nation's "infrastructure." In addition, although millions of new jobs had been created in the years before Bush's election, many of them paid very low wages.

For many years, the United States had spent huge amounts of money on its military forces. Other nations, such as Japan and Germany, had invested more of their money in their industries and social systems. Because of this, American businesses were having serious trouble competing with foreign businesses.

In the 1980's, President Reagan had spent hundreds of billions of dollars on the military while cutting taxes. This created a budget deficit of a size never before seen. In other words, the United States government spent more, took in less, and borrowed the difference. The government has borrowed money from wealthy Americans and corporations as well as from foreign governments and corporations. The money the government owes is called the "national debt." In eight years under President Reagan, the government ran up a larger national debt than had all previous presidents together.

The next generation of Americans would have to pay the growing national debt and pay the huge and growing interest on the debt. The worst part of this was that money used to pay

The Deficit and the National Debt

Estimates of budget deficit and national debt in 1992:

1992 deficit	$334 billion
Total national debt	$4 trillion
Amount the federal government borrowed per minute	$700,000
Each American's share of the national debt	$16,000

Accumulation of the national debt:

From George Washington through Jimmy Carter	$1.1 trillion
Under Ronald Reagan and George Bush	$3 trillion
Amount of every $100 paid in federal income tax that went to pay interest on the national debt in 1960	$9
Amount of every $100 paid in federal income tax that went to pay interest on the national debt in 1991	$29

Debt accumulated by recent administrations:

Bush	$1.3 trillion
Reagan	$1.8 trillion
Carter	$0.3 trillion
Ford	$0.2 trillion
Nixon	$0.1 trillion
Johnson	$0.05 trillion

the debt could not be spent on education or health care. It could not be used to rebuild the decaying cities or to replace outdated technology. As he prepared to take the oath of office, George Bush knew that he faced many challenges.

Chapter 7

The New World Order

George Bush was sworn in as United States president on January 20, 1989. In his inaugural address, he spoke of a "new breeze" ending totalitarianism overseas and bringing a kinder, gentler nation at home. Did this "new breeze" mean that Bush would step out of Reagan's shadow to set his own course for the nation? Observers analyzed every Bush action or word for insight into what he intended.

In truth, Bush wanted to improve the management of existing government programs and to be prepared to deal with whatever sudden crises might endanger the nation. He would not try to bend the country to fit a vision he brought to office. The real Bush was not an ideologue, as was Ronald Reagan. He did not have an extensive list of new programs, as Franklin Roosevelt did when he took office during the Great Depression. Bush did not hunger for power, as had some presidents, such as Lyndon Johnson and Richard Nixon. Bush's essential quality was that of noblesse oblige—the desire to serve his country.

After the 1988 election, many political analysts predicted trouble for the Bush presidency. Democrats outnumbered Republicans in both the Senate and the House of Representatives, and many of them were furious at what they regarded as President Bush's unfair tactics against Governor Dukakis. Some observers thought that this would make it difficult for any new programs or laws to be enacted. Nonetheless, in the first three years of his administration, Bush had the most consistently high popularity ratings in recent history.

January 20, 1989: George Bush is sworn in as president of the United States. (AP/Wide World Photos)

January 20, 1989: A New President

I come before you and assume the Presidency at a moment rich with promise. We live in a peaceful, prosperous time but we can make it better. For a new breeze is blowing and a world refreshed by freedom seems reborn; for in man's heart, if not in fact, the day of the dictator is over. The totalitarian era is passing, its old ideas blown away like leaves from an ancient, lifeless tree.

My friends, we have work to do. There are the homeless, lost and roaming. There are the children who have nothing—no love, no normalcy. There are those who cannot free themselves of enslavement to whatever addiction—drugs, welfare, the demoralization that rules the slums. There is crime to be conquered, the rough crime of the streets. There are young women to be helped who are about to become mothers of children they can't care for and might not love. They need our care, our guidance and our education, though we bless them for choosing life. (from George Bush's inaugural address)

The Bush Presidential Style

Bush made himself available to the press and offered to cooperate with Democratic leaders in Congress. He set a presidential style of being friendly and open with the people.

President Bush seemed refreshingly down-to-earth. He often ran his own errands, rather than have aides do them for him. Previous presidents, when traveling around Washington with their motorcade, would often have the police stop traffic so they could go through red lights. Bush had his motorcade stop at red lights, as ordinary citizens must. The American people learned that their new president liked baseball, country music, and hunting and fishing, and that he hated broccoli. They also found that he was one of the hardest-working presidents in recent history. He got up at 5:30 A.M. to jog and was often in his office at 7:00.

Americans also liked his wife, Barbara. She seemed gentle, thoughtful, and genuine. Many Democrats and moderate Republicans thought that she was more sympathetic to their views than was her husband. For example, she caused a public uproar by admitting that, in contrast to her husband's policy, she supported banning the sale of military assault rifles to private citizens. After this controversy, she refused to take public stands on such issues. Still, many moderates and liberals believed that they had a friend in the White House.

Bush's relaxed style fit the public mood. The American people did not want great change. The country seemed prosperous and peaceful. By continuing Reagan's policies, Bush was giving the people what they wanted.

New Legislation

During his first three years in the White House, President Bush had several legislative achievements. In 1989, he signed into law a plan that would help save the savings and loan (S&L) system. It required taxpayers to pay the costs of the collapsed system, but it also provided tighter government regulation to try to prevent further such disasters.

With other legislation, Bush took steps toward the "kinder, gentler" America he had promised. The 1990 Americans with Disabilities Act was a far-reaching law that benefited millions of people. It required business and government to employ people with disabilities and to accommodate their special needs. This law expanded opportunities for 43 million disabled Americans and was the broadest expansion of civil rights since 1964.

The 1990 Clean Air Act strengthened existing antipollution standards. It required stricter emission controls on cars and factories and cleaner-burning fuels. As its provisions take effect, it will cut emissions of pollutants that cause cancer in humans and will cut down on acid rain, which destroys lakes and forests. The Civil Rights Act of 1991 strengthened protection of women and minority groups against employer discrimination. It made it easier for victims of discrimination to bring suit in court.

Bush's most damaging defeat came in late 1990, when the growing federal deficit forced him to work out a budget agreement with Congress that required new taxes. Many Republican conservatives were angry when he broke his famous campaign pledge: "Read my lips, no new taxes." Nevertheless, the American people generally liked Bush, and his popularity remained high for three years.

During the third year of his presidency, however, a recession hit the nation, and it gradually grew worse. Unemployment rose, and many people feared that they might be next to lose their jobs. With the economy stagnant, people began to demand change. In 1992 Bush was forced to search for new approaches to the growing problems in the United States. This part of being president was not one with which Bush was comfortable. He had always viewed the president's job as primarily being concerned with international affairs. Yet even in that arena, things were no longer as Bush had always known them to be.

The Cold War: The "Old" World Order

George Bush's view of the world had been shaped by the Cold War. In the 1940's, World War II had forced the United States and the Soviet Union into an alliance to fight against German dictator Adolf Hitler. After Germany was defeated in 1945, the Americans and Soviets could not sustain their friendship. The long era of the Cold War began. These two powerful nations divided the world into countries that were friendly either to one or to the other. For half a century they used political, economic, and sometimes military action to try to weaken each other. The United States poured money and arms into friendly nations in order to build an economic and military barrier around what was called the "Soviet bloc." The Cold War shaped the thinking of every American president from Truman to Bush.

Bush had wanted to be president partly because he believed that he was the best person to direct Cold War strategy. He regarded the world as a huge chessboard. When something threatened a piece, he responded coolly and efficiently, always aware that moving one chess piece altered the whole board. An example of this occurred in June, 1989. The Communist government of China used force to crush a democratic uprising in the capital city of Beijing. Hundreds of unarmed demonstrators in Tiananmen Square were massacred by the Chinese army. Many Americans angrily demanded some form of harsh retaliation against the Chinese government. Bush, however, refused to give in to such pressure. The realistic Cold War chess player knew that China was too important to world stability to isolate.

Then, however, the chessboard tipped over: The Soviet

Communist empire collapsed. In his 1990 State of the Union address, Bush said: "The events of the year just ended, the Revolution of '89 . . . marks the beginning of a new era in the world's affairs." In 1992, he said: "The biggest thing that has happened in the world in my life, in our lives, is this: By the grace of God, America won the Cold War."

Change and Challenge

In the midst of this most dramatic international change in a generation, Bush remained calm. He understood that the people in the Soviet Union and Eastern Europe were frightened and confused as their Communist governments collapsed. Bush quietly and carefully supported the emergence of new, free governments without seeming to gloat or to take advantage of their weakness.

As the Soviets moved to end the Cold War, Bush

President Bush signs the Americans with Disabilities Act (ADA) into law on the lawn of the White House in July, 1990. (AP/Wide World Photos)

established close personal relationships with Soviet President Mikhail Gorbachev and Russian President Boris Yeltsin. In several dramatic personal meetings, they signed treaties that brought about the most important arms reduction agreements in history. They sharply cut the number of nuclear weapons on both sides, especially the dangerous land-based intercontinental ballistic missiles. By the end of Bush's four years as president, the world was less dangerous than it had been on the day of his inauguration. Americans celebrated victory in the Cold War, but analysts soon realized that Bush faced a new challenge. The world order created by President Harry Truman and other visionary leaders of 1945 was gone: What new vision could Bush provide?

A New World Order

On August 2, 1990, the dictator of Iraq, Saddam Hussein, seized the tiny neighboring country of Kuwait. Bush worked to unite many nations to oppose Iraq. To gain support, he did what people had long criticized him for not doing: He enunciated a vision. He envisioned a "new world order," he said, of peace and harmony, based on prosperity, democracy, and the rule of law.

There were problems in defining exactly what the new world order would be. Increasing numbers of Americans realized that the United States had to use more of its money and energy to rebuild its own economic and social structure instead of continuing to spend vast amounts to "police" the world. If the United States was not going to continue its dominating role in the new order, what would take its place? Part of the answer, President Bush hoped, would be the United Nations. That organization had been weakened by the division of the world during the Cold War. Perhaps now world leaders could begin to strengthen it to make it an effective collective force for world harmony.

Chapter 8

Challenges to the New World Order

The new world order proclaimed by President Bush would be defined by his actions rather than by his speeches. The two most important actions he took came in 1989 and 1991, when he used military force first against Panama, then against Iraq. His purpose, he said, was to restore the rule of law, on which the new world order would be built.

Panama and Manuel Noriega

Panama is a tiny country in central America. In 1989, Panama had been controlled for eight years by Manuel Noriega. Noriega, born in Panama, grew up without parents in one of the poorest slums in the world. In 1958 Noriega became an informer for the American CIA. He had once dreamed of going to medical school, but now money and power became his goals. The CIA trained him in spying and put him on its payroll. He even had private meetings with CIA director George Bush in the 1970's. In 1981 Noriega took over Panama, using a succession of presidents as fronts behind which he ruled. During the Reagan administration, he became increasingly important to Washington. In 1981 alone, he was paid $180,000 by U.S. intelligence-gathering agencies.

Noriega, however, was loyal to no one. While he worked for the American CIA, he also took money from the intelligence services of at least ten other nations. He turned over some drug dealers to the American Drug Enforcement Administration (DEA), but he also became involved in drug trafficking himself. He established his own connections with a huge Colombian drug ring, the Medellin cartel.

In the mid-1980's, Noriega's criminal activities were investigated by the U.S. Congress. Federal grand juries in Tampa and Miami finally indicted Noriega for drug trafficking in early 1988. Noriega remained in power, however, and became an increasing embarrassment to the U.S. government. Several clashes occurred between Noriega's troops and American citizens in Panama. In one case they detained and beat a young Navy officer and threatened his wife.

In late December, 1989, President Bush acted. He ordered an invasion of Panama by 24,000 American troops. After several days of sporadic fighting, Noriega surrendered. United States officials took him to Florida for trial. In 1992 Noriega was convicted of drug crimes and sentenced to forty years in prison.

Any action by a president is closely examined and criticized. Most Americans were happy about the removal of Noriega. However, although President Bush called the invasion Operation Just Cause, there were some who wondered whether it had been justified. The operation killed more than twenty Americans and hundreds of Panamanians, including many civilians. The action also raised a serious question—one that would be asked again after the war against Iraq in 1991: If someone is so evil that an invasion becomes necessary to remove him, then why did the United States help build him up in the first place?

Iraq and Saddam Hussein

Iraq, in the Middle East, shares long borders with Iran, Syria, and Saudi Arabia. It also shares a border with tiny Kuwait. All of these countries are important oil-producing nations. In 1991 Saddam Hussein was the dictator of Iraq; he had been in control of the country for twelve years. The poverty and misery that the orphan Saddam had experienced growing up in Iraq was worse than anything Noriega had faced. In 1957, at age twenty, he joined the revolutionary Baath party, which used violence as a political weapon. Saddam Hussein rose to power in an atmosphere of danger and

At his Kennebunkport home in August, 1990, Bush talks with reporters about Iraq's invasion of Kuwait. (AP/Wide World Photos)

brutality. After he took control of Iraq in 1979, he ruthlessly crushed any opposition to his rule.

Hussein began to modernize Iraq. He used its oil wealth to try to develop economic diversity and to improve Iraq's educational and health systems. Unfortunately, a long and costly war with neighboring Iran destroyed much of his good work for the Iraqi people. Because Iran and the United States were bitter enemies, the U.S. quietly helped Hussein when he went to war with Iran. The Reagan and Bush administrations sent billions of dollars of aid to Iraq during the bloody war. Any good will that Hussein had developed with the American government, however, vanished suddenly when he took over Kuwait.

Iraq Invades Kuwait

On August 2, 1990, television and radio announced to the world that Iraq had invaded Kuwait. Within a few hours, Iraqi forces had taken over the country. Why did Saddam Hussein invade Kuwait? Kuwait, long ruled by the al-Sabah family, floated on oil, making it one of the richest countries on earth. Hussein was angry at Kuwait after his expensive war with Iran. He believed that his war had helped protect Kuwait from Iran and that Kuwait had provided little support. He demanded that Kuwait allow Iraq not to pay back a loan and allow Iraq to take some Kuwaiti territory that both countries claimed. Kuwait refused.

Hussein was brutal and ruthless. Scenting weakness in Kuwait and guessing, incorrectly, that the United States would not stop him, he grabbed Kuwait and its immense oil fields. President Bush did not seem very concerned on the morning of the invasion. At first he told reporters that he was not planning on taking any action in the Persian Gulf. Bush telephoned several Arab leaders. King Hussein of Jordan urged the United States not to get involved, but to allow an "Arab solution." The king warned Bush that if Saddam Hussein were threatened, he would not leave. Saddam, he said, had been surrounded by enemies since he was a child and did not frighten easily.

Later in the day, however, Bush's thinking took a crucial turn. He remembered World War II, when many nations united and stood firm against Hitler's Germany. It seemed to him that Saddam Hussein was an evil force like Hitler. There could be no room for compromise with such a person. Bush later told advisers: "I've had a lot of time to think about the situation in the Middle East, I've reconciled all the moral issues. It's black versus white, good versus evil." Bush rejected King Hussein's plea for an Arab solution. He told reporters: "This will not stand. This will not stand, this aggression against Kuwait."

Bush had always seen foreign relations as his strong point, and now he swung into action. In one of the most skillful diplomatic campaigns in the post-World War II era, Bush put together a global coalition against Iraq. He even did what many experts thought was impossible: He got support from most Arab nations for the United States' policy against Iraq, their Arab neighbor. The key was King Fahd of the oil-rich nation of Saudi Arabia. Saudi Arabia was particularly important within the Arab world because it was the focal point of the religion of Islam. The founder of Islam, Muhammad,

PERSIAN GULF REGION

had lived there in the holy city of Mecca. Bush convinced King Fahd that Saddam Hussein intended to invade his kingdom next.

President Bush then took the American case to the United Nations. The U.N. passed resolutions calling on Iraq to withdraw from Kuwait. It imposed economic sanctions to isolate Iraq and authorized the use of force if Iraqi troops did not withdraw. Through it all, Hussein refused to leave Kuwait. He promised to cover the desert sand with blood in the "mother of all battles" if his troops were attacked.

Desert Storm

Bush also had to line up support among his own American military commanders. Many of these leaders believed that Washington had abandoned them during the Vietnam War in the late 1960's and early 1970's. They wanted never again to use military power unless the nation committed itself with overwhelming force and with the intention to win. Military leaders gave that message to commander-in-chief Bush, and the old bomber pilot agreed. Bush sent about 540,000 American troops to the Persian Gulf region, most of them

---

Bush and Hussein: A War of Words

The valiant Iraqi men and women will not allow the army of atheism, treachery, hypocrisy and [word indistinct] to realize their stupid hope that the war would only last a few days and weeks. . . . When they begin to die and when the message of the Iraqi soldiers reaches the farthest corner of the world, the unjust will die and the "God is Great" banner will flutter with great victory in the mother of all battles. (Saddam Hussein, January 20, 1991)

The community of nations has resolutely gathered to condemn and repel lawless aggression. Saddam Hussein's unprovoked invasion—his ruthless, systematic rape of a peaceful neighbor—violated everything the community of nations holds dear. The world has said this aggression would not stand, and it will not stand. (George Bush: State of the Union address, January 29, 1991)

based in Saudi Arabia. The huge movement of personnel and equipment was called Operation Desert Shield.

Saddam Hussein still did not withdraw, and on January 16, 1991, the United Nations' forces attacked. Desert Shield became Operation Desert Storm. American troops led the attack. The war lasted only forty-three days. Iraqi troops, overwhelmed by the firepower of the opposing forces, fought poorly. Nearly 150 Americans died in action. Figures on Iraqi deaths vary widely, but a huge number of Iraqi soldiers and civilians died—probably more than 100,000 people. After Iraqi troops left Kuwait, Bush halted the war. Kuwait was officially liberated on February 27, 1991. Saddam Hussein remained in power in Iraq.

The meaning of the war began to be debated soon after it ended. Some critics claimed that it was unnecessary, insisting that Hussein would have withdrawn peacefully if Bush had not intervened. The war caused tremendous death, destruction, and hardship for the Iraqi people, many of them innocent civilians. Some critics also argued that if Hussein were so evil, Washington should not have helped him become so powerful in the first place—and should not have left him in power after his defeat.

Others believed that the war represented a healthy recovery from the "Vietnam syndrome," the reluctance of the United States to become involved in military operations for fear of being bogged down in an endless war. They praised the effectiveness of the United States' expensive, high-technology weapons. Some supporters regarded the Gulf War as the beginning of a definition of a new world order. It showed, they said, that the world community would no longer tolerate aggression by one nation against another.

Chapter 9

The Trials of 1992

Good fortune smiled on George Bush in the early years of his presidency, and it was reflected in national polls of his popularity. In the first half of 1991, for example, after the Gulf War, his approval rating reached a high in the 80 percent range. Many political experts concluded that Bush could not be defeated in the upcoming 1992 election.

In mid-1991, however, Bush's popularity began the biggest plunge in polling history. Bush fell in public esteem because of a recession that began in 1990 and continued through 1991 and into 1992. Millions of Americans lost their jobs. The recession spread gloom throughout the nation. Many of those who retained good jobs worried about their own future and that of their children. Suddenly, achievements that would have brought the president acclaim in the past were almost ignored as increasingly pessimistic Americans turned their attention from the international scene to problems at home.

Diplomatic Achievements

In 1991 and 1992, Bush began several foreign policy initiatives that the next generation may regard as major events in the post-World War II era. For example, in August, 1991, Bush and Soviet President Mikhail Gorbachev signed a treaty that provided for a 30-percent reduction in long-range nuclear missiles. In June, 1992, Bush and Russian President Boris Yeltsin agreed to eliminate completely the most dangerous types of missiles and to reduce drastically each nation's stockpile of all types of nuclear weapons.

In another major achievement, Bush moved to protect the

long-range American economic position. He realized that there
was a danger that in the future the United States might be
excluded from the European and Asian economic markets. In
the fall of 1992, American, Mexican, and Canadian leaders
agreed to the North American Free Trade Agreement. This
agreement would eliminate trade barriers among the three
nations, creating the largest free trade zone in the world. It
would provide a secure trade base for the United States in an
increasingly competitive world.

Another major initiative involved the Middle East. Conflict
between Israel and its Arab neighbors had been continuous
since Israel became a nation in 1948. There was always the
danger that this regional conflict would pull the superpowers,
who backed opposing sides, into a global war. Every president
since Harry Truman had tried and failed to bring peace to the
Middle East. In 1991 and 1992, Bush and Secretary of State
James Baker began a Middle Eastern peace process that
showed promise in bringing peace to that troubled region and
making the whole world safer. Because of United States
pressure and persuasion, both sides began serious discussion of
the issues that divided them, and each side began to offer
meaningful concessions to the other.

The Los Angeles Riot

Although the nation's poor economy was the central
problem President Bush faced in 1992, other events added to a
feeling that he was not providing the leadership America
needed. Two of these were the Los Angeles riot and the United
Nations' international conference on the environment that was
held in Rio de Janeiro, Brazil.

The spark that ignited the Los Angeles riot was the verdict
in a trial in which police officers were accused of using
excessive force against a black man. In the early morning of
March 3, 1991, Los Angeles police stopped a motorist named

A shopping mall burning in Los Angeles on April 30, 1992, the second day of the rioting.
(AP/Wide World Photos)

Rodney King. Unknown to the police, an onlooker videotaped them beating King while he writhed on the ground. For months afterward, television news shows all over the country replayed slow-motion scenes of the white officers beating a defenseless black man.

Four police officers were arrested for using undue force. They were tried in the affluent white community of Simi Valley, near Los Angeles. On April 29, 1992, a stunned nation learned that the jury, which included no blacks, had acquitted the officers. A few hours later in Los Angeles, shock gave way to rage. The worst racial disturbance in American history began. In three days, it left more than fifty people dead and thousands of buildings burned. Shocking scenes of what looked like a whole city in flames were broadcast throughout the country.

Although the verdict in the police beating of King was the immediate reason for the rioting, there were deeper underlying causes. Many Americans did not like to face these issues, but there were great inequalities in education, jobs, and wealth in the country.

After World War II, many middle-class people moved from the cities to the new suburbs. As jobs also moved out to the suburbs, the cities became poorer and poorer. The cities soon faced problems they could not afford to fix: growing crime and drug problems, decaying streets and bridges, and poor schools. Federal aid to the cities declined from $47.2 billion in 1980 to $21.7 billion in 1990. Because it was mostly white people who could afford to move to the suburbs, a high proportion of minorities lived in the troubled inner cities. Although millions of minority people throughout the country lived in stable families with good incomes and no problems with school or drugs, millions of others faced terrible poverty. Black and Hispanic families, especially, were under tremendous pressure. Millions of people saw no escape from the slums where they lived.

The King verdict horrified most Americans. Yet President Bush, wanting calm, did not respond to their outrage. He said: "The court system has worked. What's needed now is calm and respect for the law." Many Americans felt that Bush's reaction missed the point. They believed that the court system had not worked properly and that respect for law had resulted in injustice. Later, Bush said that the verdict had actually stunned him, and he announced that the Justice Department would attempt to indict the four police officers in federal court for violating Rodney King's civil rights. Yet the impression of his initial inaction lingered, as did the haunting images of looting and an American city in flames.

The Rio Conference

The Los Angeles riot cast doubt on Bush's vision of a kinder, gentler nation. He had also promised in 1988 to be the "environmental president," and he did make some environmental gains. The Clean Air Act, for example, tightened pollution controls. Yet many environmentalists believed that the Bush administration was not enforcing environmental laws strongly.

In June, 1992, representatives of more than a hundred nations met at Rio de Janeiro for the United Nations Conference on Environment and Development. Thousands of the world's political and environmental leaders met to discuss scientific research on the environment and to formulate plans to deal with global problems.

The conference faced a bewildering array of complex issues. Growing concern for protecting the world's environment was coming face to face with economic realities. The world's wealthy, industrialized nations had developed at a time when no one had worried about pollution or the environment. Now, the rich countries wanted to impose strict environmental controls on poor, developing countries. Such regulations would hold the poorer countries back. The nations of the world were trying to find ways to protect the environment without forcing poor countries to remain in poverty.

President Bush, although proclaiming himself the environmental president, actually believed in moving slowly on environmental issues. He sometimes dismissed environmentalists as the "spotted owl crowd." Bush was concerned that business should not be hurt by environmental restrictions. Knowing that the Rio conference would involve controversy, at first he had not even wanted to attend.

The conference resulted in some important gains. Participants exchanged information, established environmental priorities, and signed treaties, such as an agreement to reduce emissions of greenhouse gases (gases that cause global warming). Bush, however, was not a leader at the conference. He refused to sign one major treaty (the biodiversity treaty) that was signed by more than 120 nations. Bush's actions allowed his critics to claim that he was giving environmental concerns a cold shoulder. For example, he only signed the treaty to reduce greenhouse gases after other nations agreed to weaken it by removing specific targets and timetables.

The 1992 Election

In mid-1991, it had seemed to most political observers that Bush would be unbeatable in the upcoming election. Yet in October, 1991, a Bush pollster found a disturbing trend. Although Bush remained popular, a sense of gloom was spreading among the American people. The United States economy was in a recession, and half the people polled believed that the nation was on the "wrong course." This trend was potentially disastrous for Bush, because for three years his message had been that the nation needed no change in direction. By the end of 1991, Bush had fallen drastically in popularity polls. The problems of the economy damaged his standing. Breaking his "no-new-taxes" pledge had also hurt him with conservatives in his party.

Conservatives found a voice when journalist Pat Buchanan, who had never held elective office, led a revolt from within the president's own party. In January, 1992, Buchanan shocked the White House by getting nearly 40 percent of the Republican vote in the New Hampshire primary. He continued to run well in several later primaries. With a large minority in Bush's own party wanting a change, some advisers realized that the president was in serious trouble with the electorate.

Bush, however, did not seem worried by such predictions. At first he simply sought to reassure voters that the economic situation was not as bad as reported. Moreover, he did not organize his campaign early, and he waited until after the Republican Convention in August to campaign in earnest. He did not describe a clear economic program that might inspire the country's worried voters. As the months passed, the campaign reaffirmed an old rule of politics: American voters pay little attention to foreign affairs when the economy is in trouble. The military victory of Desert Storm seemed to have faded from people's minds.

Many major Democratic politicians had decided in 1991 not to run against Bush because he seemed unbeatable. Their absence made it possible for a new generation of young leaders to move forward. Bill Clinton, the governor of Arkansas, emerged in the spring of 1992 as the front-runner of that group. His record in bringing progress to Arkansas, one of the poorest states, brought hope to many Americans troubled about the nation's future. Most important, no other candidate had such a comprehensive set of recommendations to deal with the crisis of the 1990's.

American politics is usually called a "two-party system." In rare elections, however, a third candidate or party emerges with enough enthusiasm and support to be taken seriously as a

Democrat Bill Clinton (left) and independent candidate H. Ross Perot, Bush's opponents in the 1992 presidential campaign. (AP/Wide World Photos)

political force. The 1992 election was one of those. Discontent fueled a third-party revolt behind a Texas billionaire named H. Ross Perot. At times, early in the race, Perot surprisingly led both Bush and Clinton in the polls.

By summer, polls clearly showed Clinton ahead of Bush. In July, the Democratic Convention officially nominated Clinton as its candidate and Tennessee Senator Al Gore as his running mate. Then, in a surprise move, Perot suddenly withdrew from the race while the Democratic Convention was being held. In a *Time*-CNN poll taken shortly after the convention, Clinton led Bush 53 percent to 26 percent.

Bush was in a bind. By 1992 the American people wanted change. Reagan-Bush policies had been in place for twelve years, however, so Bush could not credibly put himself forward as an agent of change. During the Republican Convention in August, controversies over abortion rights and policies toward gays and minorities distracted Bush and the party at a time when he needed to unite a coalition of voters behind him. As the convention ended, Bush remained far behind Clinton in the polls.

Bush stressed his foreign policy achievements; he launched tough attacks on Clinton's record and on his character. Nothing seemed to work. Political messages and techniques that had worked in the 1988 campaign were apparently having no effect in 1992. Week after week, Clinton led by a wide margin in the polls. In late September, another surprise occurred: Perot reentered the race.

Perhaps Bush's best chance at stopping Clinton's momentum was in three televised face-to-face debates. Yet as it turned out, the debates had little effect on the campaign. Neither Clinton nor Bush made a serious mistake or landed a disabling verbal blow. Perot also participated in the debates, and he focused most of his attacks on Bush. After the debates, Clinton was still ahead.

In the last days of the campaign, it seemed that the barrage
of Republican attacks on Clinton might finally be paying off.
Polls showed Bush narrowing Clinton's lead. Perot also was
gaining in the polls and seemed to be draining support from
Clinton. Clinton's advisers were worried; victory, they feared,
might be slipping away. Perot's campaign suddenly faltered,
however, when he publicly made bizarre and unsubstantiated
allegations of Republican "dirty tricks" aimed at his family.
Bush's last-minute surge also faded. Through it all, Clinton
worked tirelessly. He had run an effective campaign. He
responded immediately to any new Bush attack, and he kept
his campaign theme focused on the need for change, especially
in economic policy. On November 3, Clinton won 43 percent
of the popular vote, compared with 38 percent for Bush and 19
percent for Perot.

After the Election

Days after the end of the sometimes bitter election
campaign, Bush and Clinton put it behind them and began to
work together. Bush began one of his last major services to the
nation: He helped create a smooth transition of power,
preparing the new president to take office on January 20, 1993.
As Bush reminded his supporters in his concession speech on
election day, "America must always come first."

In the first days after the election, Bush did not appear in
public often. The nation's attention was focused on
president-elect Bill Clinton. George and Barbara Bush went on
a fishing vacation to Florida. Soon, however, events brought
Bush into the public eye again. One event was personal: On
November 19, Dorothy Bush, who had been such a strong
influence on her son, died in Greenwich, Connecticut, at the
age of ninety-one. A saddened President Bush joined other
family members at her funeral.

Another event was both political and tragic. In the African

country of Somalia, a famine was killing thousands of people by the end of 1992. In November, American television showed horrifying scenes of mass starvation. Emergency food was not getting to the people who needed it, because warlords and marauders were stealing it. The situation in Somalia was chaotic. The country's government had fallen apart.

Bush considered what could be done. In December, he announced that he would send American troops to Somalia to do "God's work"—to help safeguard and distribute food supplies. In the second week of December, U.S. forces landed to begin the mission, officially named "Operation Restore Hope."

Bush flew to Somalia to visit the troops at work at the beginning of January, 1993. From Somalia he flew to Moscow, where he and Boris Yeltsin had arranged to sign the second Strategic Arms Reduction Talks treaty, or START II. This was the most sweeping agreement in history to reduce nuclear weapons. Both leaders hailed the treaty, saying that it promised a less fearful future for the entire world. Under the agreement, Russia and the United States agreed to cut their arsenals of strategic nuclear weapons by two-thirds by the year 2003.

Looking Back and Looking Ahead

Shortly after the election, there had been speculation that Bush was suffering from depression, but he never publicly displayed such emotions. Naturally enough, he did admit being disappointed by the outcome. Yet at the time of the election Bush was sixty-eight, an age when many Americans have already retired. He could look back on many years of service to his country. He could also look ahead. He would have time to pursue his interests in sports such as fishing and golf. He would also be able to spend more time with his large family. As he put it, he looked forward to getting into "the grandparent business."

Chapter 10

Legacy

President Bush's place in history will be clearer to future generations, when controversies of the moment have been forgotten. When President Truman left office in 1953, for example, his popularity ratings were the lowest ever recorded for a president, before or since. Yet by the 1970's, he was regarded as one of the nation's best presidents. Many Bush admirers believe that time will treat him well. His critics, on the other hand, believe that his reluctance to deal with problems within the United States will be viewed unfavorably.

Measuring Greatness

Presidents take different paths to greatness. George Washington and Abraham Lincoln guided the nation through times of crisis. Thomas Jefferson left a legacy of ideas that defined national purpose. Theodore Roosevelt laid out a public policy path that later presidents followed. Andrew Jackson and Woodrow Wilson successfully guided the nation through periods of social and economic transition. Franklin Roosevelt's greatness is based on major legislative and foreign policy accomplishments.

In measuring presidential achievement, people usually rate highly presidents associated with change. For this reason, conservative presidents such as George Bush face a problem in terms of their place in history. "Conservative" comes from the word "conserve." It implies an intention to maintain the status quo—to keep things as they are—rather than to bring about change. Yet some conservatives are associated with change. Ronald Reagan was one such conservative. He wanted change because he believed that the nation was on the wrong path. He directed his powerful conservative vision toward returning to older governmental patterns instead of creating new ones.

George Bush was a more traditional conservative. He inherited the status quo passed on to him by Reagan, and he announced at the beginning of the 1988 campaign that he saw no need for change. He did not push further along Reagan's path, nor did he turn from that path in any dramatic fashion.

Bush saw his task as administering competently the domestic and foreign policies he inherited. Such conservative

President Bush gives his first State of the Union address. Behind him are Vice President Dan Quayle (left) and House Speaker Thomas Foley (right). (AP/Wide World Photos)

presidents can be judged successes if they do this well. They
may be judged failures either if they are poor managers or if
their times call for change that they are unable to provide.
Dwight Eisenhower, president from 1953 to 1961, was a
conservative president who skillfully administered the policies
he inherited and coped reasonably well with changing times.

A Model Life

Presidents are often regarded as important models for young
people, and George Bush provided a traditional model of
behavior and values. His life reinforced the values and the
promise embodied in the work ethic: Hard work, morality, and
frugality will be rewarded by success. A young man of his
class could have rested on his family's wealth and position.
Bush did not. Hard work was one of his primary characteristics.

Bush also exemplified the meaning of noblesse oblige, a
traditional Establishment value. He felt a deep need to serve
society. He thought in terms of mission. When he began a
mission—whether to fly a slow bomber into enemy fire, to
serve a president loyally, or to remove Iraqi forces from
Kuwait—nothing deterred him. Bush had little interest in
power for its own sake. His mission to serve, mixed with a
healthy amount of ambition and desire for power, pushed him
forward in public life.

George and Barbara Bush embodied other traditional
values: the family, religion, and patriotism. As a conservative,
Bush had little faith in the ability of government to solve the
nation's social problems. He believed that solutions rested on
strong families passing along traditional religious morality and
love of country to their children.

The Presidency

Many recent presidencies, among them those of Richard
Nixon and Ronald Reagan, have been marked by abuse of

power or corruption. Bush set a style of openness for his administration and was proud of the ethical standard that he set. He did not seem interested in using his office to pursue and punish his enemies. By the end of his presidency, only minor instances of wrongdoing had become public. One example involved Bush's chief of staff, John Sununu, who resigned partly because he abused government travel regulations by having taxpayers pay for his personal expenses.

Bush administered the programs that he inherited, and he was generally successful in putting capable men and women in charge of departments and major agencies and then leaving them alone to do their work. Yet, although Bush probably managed the executive branch about as well as that huge institution can be managed, he did not quell the public's increasing disaffection with government. The anger that fed the 1992 candidacy of Ross Perot was directed at the ineffectiveness of the president and Congress in coping with the crisis of the 1990's.

Domestic Policy

Conservative presidents are effective and valuable to the nation when the policy they administer fits the times. They face disaster, however, if they cannot adjust to changing circumstances. Bush achieved some of his domestic goals: a stronger civil rights law to protect women and minority groups, the strongest law in history to protect disabled Americans, and new environmental laws, especially to improve air quality.

Despite these achievements, however, President Bush found it difficult to deal with the economic recession and to confront the deeper problems of the 1990's. He was hampered by the Reagan legacy of low spending on social programs. The huge federal budget deficit limited his ability to strike out in new directions to solve mounting problems in the economy.

Remaining loyal to the former president's vision, he could not formulate a way to resolve the country's economic crisis.

Foreign Policy

George Bush would probably list his major achievement as putting before the world community the vision of a "new world order." That order, he said, must be based on democracy and prosperity. It must follow the rule of law instead of the law of the jungle. President Bush was criticized for not giving substance to his conception of the new world order, but new eras of history are not born easily. Often people do not even realize that an era has ended until long afterward. It may take many years before the major characteristics of a new era are recognized.

Bush could argue that he began to give substance to his vision through his actions in Panama and Kuwait: By removing Manuel Noriega from power, Bush said that international criminal activities would not be tolerated; by expelling Saddam Hussein's forces from Kuwait, he defined the new world order to exclude aggression of one state against another.

Bush and Secretary of State James Baker worked hard and made progress toward settling the age-old conflict between Israel and the Arab nations. Bush improved relations with the Arabs, headed off attempts by Congress to impose harsh sanctions on China because of the Tienanmen Square massacre, and fought against "Japanese bashing" by politicians trying to take advantage of public fears of a declining American economy.

Many questions remained to be answered. Would the United States continue to "police" the world, as it had done in Panama, or would it act in concert with other great powers in rebuilding the United Nations to play the peacekeeping role for which it had been designed. What did the future hold for the former Soviet republics? Could the great industrial powers cooperate in building a world economic system that would benefit all, or would the United States engage in an economic war with Japan, Germany, and other nations?

Yet although questions remained, it seemed that the most dangerous period in world history had ended. Bush helped ease the nation into a new era, and he began to define some of its contours by his actions in Panama and the Persian Gulf. His message to the nation was that Americans had to learn to live in a new age. The new world order was one in which—for the first time in half a century—the American people could live free of the fear that international conflict could unleash a nuclear holocaust.

Soviet president Mikhail Gorbachev and George Bush signed a historic agreement to reduce nuclear weapons. (AP/Wide World Photos)

Achievements

Achievement	Year	Description
Texas politician	1962-1971	After World War II, the Republican Party experienced dynamic growth in the South and Southwest. Bush was one of the young leaders in this rebirth of Republicanism.
United States ambassador to the United Nations	1971-1972	Bush's U.N. ambassadorship introduced him to international affairs, which became his specialty for the rest of his career.
Director of Central Intelligence Agency	1976	The CIA, in 1976, was battered by charges of incompetence and illegal operations. Bush set an open, forthcoming style that helped the agency regain its status. He also rebuilt morale within the CIA.
The vice presidency	1981-1989	Bush won the trust of President Reagan, who made him an important member of his administration. Few, if any, previous vice presidents had as important a role in the upper levels of an administration.
Panama invasion	1989	In December, 1989, Bush ordered the invasion of Panama to remove dictator and drug trafficker Manuel Noriega from power.
Legislation	1989-1991	Bush signed important pieces of legislation into law, including the 1990 Americans with Disabilities Act, and 1990 Clean Air Act, and the 1991 Civil Rights Act.

The end of the Cold War	1989-1993	The Cold War began to wind down during the 1980's. Even skeptics finally admitted that the Cold War was over during the third year of the Bush administration, when the Soviet Union collapsed.
The new world order	1989-1993	As the Cold War ended, Bush put forward the idea of a "new world order," a community based on peace and the "rule of law."
Persian Gulf War	1990-1991	Bush assembled an international coalition that forced Iraqi dictator Saddam Hussein to withdraw his troops from Kuwait.
Middle East diplomacy	1991-1993	Bush and Secretary of State James Baker succeeded in bringing Israel and its Arab neighbors together to begin peace talks. Although progress was slow, the very fact that negotiations had begun was significant.
Nuclear arms reduction	1991-1993	Bush signed treaties with Soviet President Mikhail Gorbachev, then with Russian President Boris Yeltsin, to reduce the nuclear stockpiles of the superpowers. Major agreements were signed in 1991 and 1993 (the START II treaty).

Time Line

1924 *June 12.* George Herbert Walker Bush is born in Milton, Massachusetts.

1925 *June 8.* Barbara Pierce is born.

1936 George Bush starts prep school at Phillips Academy (Andover, Massachusetts).

1941 George Bush and Barbara Pierce meet.

1942 *December.* Bush enlists in the Navy.

1944 *June 19.* Bush is shot down and quickly rescued.

   September 2. He is shot down over Chichi Jima.

1945 *January 6.* Bush marries Barbara (Pierce) Bush.

   Bush receives Navy discharge and enters Yale University.

1946 George Walker, the first of six Bush children is born; the others are Pauline Robinson "Robin" (1949), John Ellis (1953), Neil Mallon (1955), Marvin Pierce (1956), and Dorothy Walker (1959).

1948 Bush graduates from Yale University, then moves to Texas and works for Dresser Industries.

1951 Bush establishes Bush-Overbey oil firm.

1953 Bush helps establish, and becomes vice president of, Zapata Petroleum; daughter Robin dies of leukemia.

1959 Bush becomes head of his own company, Zapata Off-Shore.

1962 Bush becomes chair of Harris County Republican Party.

1964 Bush runs for United States Senate and is defeated by Ralph Yarborough.

1966 Bush sells Zapata Off-Shore; in November, he is elected to the House of Representatives.

1968 Bush wins reelection to House of Representatives.

1970 Bush runs for the United States Senate; he is defeated by Lloyd Bentsen.

1971 Bush becomes United States Ambassador to the United Nations.

1972 Bush's father, Prescott Bush, dies.

1973 Bush becomes chair of the Republican National Committee.

1974	Bush informs Richard Nixon that he must resign from the presidency; Bush becomes American envoy to People's Republic of China.
1975	*November.* Bush is asked by President Ford to become director of the Central Intelligence Agency (CIA).
1976	*January.* Bush is confirmed by the Senate as director of the CIA.
1977	*January.* Bush reenters private life.
1979	*May 1.* Bush announces that he will seek the 1980 Republican nomination for the presidency.
1980	Ronald Reagan defeats Bush for the Republican nomination; Bush is chosen by Reagan as vice presidential nominee; in November, Bush is elected vice president.
1981	*January 20.* Bush is inaugurated vice president of the United States.
	March. Reagan is shot and wounded in an assassination attempt.
1984	*November.* Bush is reelected vice president.
1985	The Iran-Contra conspiracy becomes public.
1988	The savings and loan industry verges on collapse; Bush wins the Republican nomination for the presidency.
	November 8. Bush is elected president.
1989	*January 20.* Bush is inaugurated as president.
	December. Bush orders invasion of Panama and seizure of Manuel Noriega.
1990	Bush signs into law two important acts: the Americans with Disabilities Act and the Clean Air Act; Bush breaks his "no-new-taxes" pledge.
	August 2. Iraq invades Kuwait.
1991	*January 16.* Bush orders Desert Storm military action against Iraq.
	February 27. Bush announces that Kuwait is liberated and Iraq defeated.
	December. Mikhail Gorbachev falls from power in the Soviet Union.
1992	*January.* Bush proclaims a United States victory in the Cold War.
	Spring. Bill Clinton (Democrat) and H. Ross Perot (independent) emerge as Bush's opponents in the presidential race.
	April. The Los Angeles riot occurs.

1992   *August.* Bush wins the Republican nomination for the presidency.

        November. Bill Clinton wins the presidential election.

        December. Bush orders American troops into Somalia to safeguard efforts to relieve widespread starvation.

1993   *January.* Russian President Boris Yeltsin and George Bush sign the START II arms-reduction treaty.

Glossary

Budget deficit: The shortfall that occurs when the federal government's tax revenues fail to pay fully the costs of government operations; the government then pays the deficit by borrowing money and adding to the national debt.

Central Intelligence Agency (CIA): A government organization established in 1947 to coordinate American intelligence gathering, or "spying"; it gathers information about foreign nations and sometimes conducts secret operations in those countries.

Civil rights: Rights guaranteed to all citizens, such as the right to vote or to receive equal treatment from public institutions; in recent years the term most often refers to efforts to protect the civil rights of minority people.

Cold War: An international situation that existed from about 1945 to 1991, when the United States and the Soviet Union divided the world; they attempted to weaken each other using political and economic weapons rather than by fighting a "hot war" with military weapons.

Conservative or "right wing": A political philosophy that usually seeks to maintain (conserve) the status quo. Since World War II, the American right has generally wanted to limit government involvement in social and economic matters; conservatives generally support a strong military and want to return to what they consider traditional moral values. Conservatives are usually associated with the Republican Party, although there are many exceptions.

"Iran-Contra": A conspiracy among high government officials during the Reagan administration secretly to sell military arms to Iran and give the profits to the Contras, a group that was trying to overthrow the government of Nicaragua.

Liberal or "left wing": A political philosophy that seeks to use government power to reform or change the status quo. In recent decades, the term generally refers to those who support the reforms of Franklin D. Roosevelt's New Deal and who support programs to improve the status of minority and women. Liberals are usually associated with the Democratic Party, but there are many exceptions.

Negative campaigning: A style of campaigning in which candidates concentrate their efforts on attacking their opponents instead of explaining their own stands on the issues.

Nomination: The choosing of a candidate to run for office against the

103

nominees of the other parties; the Democratic and Republican parties each nominate their candidate at a huge national convention.

Primary election: Primaries are a part of the nomination process that occur before the national convention; state parties hold primary elections to choose a nominee of the party in that state.

Savings and Loan crisis: In the 1980's, greedy executives and managers drained billions of dollars from savings and loan institutions. President Bush's "bailout" plan saved S&L depositors by having the taxpayers assume the losses.

Voodoo economics: The term George Bush used in 1980 to describe Ronald Reagan's economic program; ironically, when Bush became president after serving as Reagan's vice president, he continued the policies he had earlier ridiculed.

Bibliography

Bush, George, with Victor Gold. *Looking Forward.* New York: Bantam Books, 1988. This Bush autobiography gives a good overview of his life up to the beginning of the 1988 campaign for the presidency. Any autobiography should be approached carefully, however, especially one written by an active politician seeking to be seen in a favorable light.

Campbell, Colin, and Bert A. Rockman, eds. *The Bush Presidency: First Appraisals.* Chatham, N.J.: Chatham House, 1991. The first scholarly study of the Bush administration. It is a collection of articles by political scientists on various aspects of the Bush presidency.

Cramer, Richard Ben. *What It Takes: The Way to the White House.* New York: Random House, 1992. An excellent book, but only for those who are fascinated by politics. It is a 1,047-page study of the 1988 election. Cramer searches for "what it takes" to get to the White House. His answer is not very reassuring. The winner, he believes, is the one most willing to be put under the control of political manipulators and to do whatever it takes to win.

Germond, Jack W., and Jules Witcover. *Whose Broad Stripes and Bright Stars?: The Trivial Pursuit of the Presidency, 1988.* New York: Warner Books, 1989. This book by two outstanding journalists provides a blow-by-blow account of the 1988 campaign. Their study is more accessible to most readers than Cramer's, but their analysis of the political system is similarly critical.

Green, Fitzhugh. *George Bush: An Intimate Portrait.* New York: Hippocrene Books, 1989. A biography based on about four hundred interviews with the Bush family and friends. Green is a friend of the family and provides a favorable portrait of Bush. Does not include his presidential years.

Grimes, Ann. *Running Mates: The Making of a First Lady.* New York: William Morrow, 1990. Focuses on the wives of the candidates who ran for presidential nomination in 1988. Grimes does not see Barbara Bush as most observers do. He portrays her as a tough political manipulator and an elitist.

Hyams, Joe. *Flight of the Avenger: George Bush at War.* New York: Harcourt Brace Jovanovich, 1991. A good description of Bush's service in World War II, written by a World War II journalist. Hyams based it on naval records and on interviews with men who served with Bush.

105

Kempe, Frederick. *Divorcing the Dictator: America's Bungled Affair with Noriega*. New York: G. P. Putnam's Sons, 1990. A good book based on interviews and government documents. Gives an interesting account of Noriega's rise to power and his long, tangled relationship with the United States. Kempe sees Noriega as corrupt but not as evil as he was portrayed in American propaganda.

Radcliffe, Donnie. *Simply Barbara Bush: A Portrait of America's Candid First Lady*. New York: Warner Books, 1989. Based on interviews with Barbara Bush and her family and friends. It is overly sweet and sympathetic, but it does let a bit of a real person peep through.

Sheehy, Gail. *Character: America's Search for Leadership*. New York: William Morrow, 1988. Sheehy provides interesting and perceptive psychological portraits of the candidates in 1988. She sees Bush as a passive person without strong beliefs; she believes that Bush displays a psychological pattern of submitting to powerful personalities, starting with his father.

Smith, Jean Edward. *George Bush's War*. New York: Henry Holt, 1992. Smith provides a short, clear, and very harsh interpretation of the Persian Gulf War. Smith believes that the war was unnecessary and was primarily brought about by Bush's need to appear strong.

Wilmsen, Steven K. *Silverado: Neil Bush and the Savings and Loan Scandal*. Washington, D.C.: National Press Books, 1991. Neil Bush, President Bush's son, was an executive at the failed Silverado Savings and Loan. Wilmsen uses the Silverado case to explore the savings and loan crisis, portraying Neil Bush as an innocent dupe. Avoids the sensationalism that tempts many authors dealing with scandals and children of the presidents.

Woodward, Bob. *The Commanders*. New York: Simon & Schuster, 1991. Woodward, perhaps the nation's most famous journalist, studied the Pentagon—the military establishment—under Bush. He had highly placed military sources that gave him information during the Panama and Persian Gulf invasions.

Media Resources

Bush Acceptance Speech. Video, 85 minutes. C-SPAN, 1988. Distributed by Purdue University Public Affairs Video Archives (to educators only). Contains some rare biographical film footage of Bush's life, as well as his complete 1988 acceptance speech to the Republican Convention, which laid the foundation for his successful campaign. Bush's 1992 acceptance speech is also available.

A Day at the White House. Video, 60 minutes. NBC News, 1990. Distributed by NBC News Archives, New York. Narrated by Tom Brokaw, this video shows how the president operates in relation to the huge White House staff. Helps viewers understand that the presidency is much bigger than a single person. Originally aired under the title *A Day in the Life of the White House*; transcripts are also available.

Frontline: The Choice '92. Video, 120 minutes. 1992. Distributed by PBS Video. Provides considerable information on the backgrounds of George Bush and Bill Clinton as well as examples and evaluations of their styles of governing. Includes many interviews, both supportive and critical of the two men. Narrated by journalist Richard Ben Cramer.

George Bush: An Intimate Portrait. Video, 60 minutes. C-SPAN, 1990. Distributed by Purdue University Public Affairs Video Archives (to educators only). A taped discussion of Bush's life by biographer Fitzhugh Green. Green's discussion is interesting partly because he himself is a member of the Eastern Establishment and an old friend of the Bush family.

The Gulf Crisis: The Road to War. Video, 136 minutes. Distributed by the American Enterprise Institute, Washington, D.C. This study has three parts: Saddam Hussein's invasion of Kuwait, the Persian Gulf War, and the implications of the action for Bush's vision of the new world order. Includes interviews with major decision makers.

World Leaders

GEORGE BUSH

INDEX